Perfectly Flawed

Virgauda Bazinova

Perfectly Flawed by Virgauda Bazinova.

Published by Lulu.com

virgaudabazinova@gmail.com.

Cover by Kristijone Kike.

Edited by Andrea Townsley.

ISBN: 978-1-312-08908-2

Printed in the United Kingdom.

Contents

Introduction

I wish that before I became a mother, someone had told me not only some of the struggles I would face when I had my own kids, but also the ways in which I could be a wiser, calmer, and truly happier mom, even in the midst of all of those struggles. I remember feeling such overwhelming joy when I first became a mom, but on the other hand, I was also taken aback by these other feelings that surfaced when things started to go differently than I had expected.

My culture and family background were shaping me both as a woman and a mother long before I really had any clue. I was born in a small town in Lithuania—in Eastern Europe—and after my parents' divorce, I was raised by my mom from the age of two. When I was only three-and-a-half years old, my mom moved us to London and I have lived here ever since. Though I grew up in England, I still embraced some of the culture of my country of birth, including learning to speak the language and joining a Lithuanian church community.

My mom re-married when I was eight, and I was really fortunate to grow up in the UK with the family, friends, and support group I developed. But I have learnt that whether your life is close to perfect or far from it, we all bring our experiences, expectations, standards, and hopes to our roles as mothers...and I was no different.

Although my life experience isn't that vast, I have still had my fair share of struggles in motherhood. If I had to choose, probably the most important thing I have learned during my journey so far, is to let go of the expectations and standards of perfection that I am upholding for myself, my family, and my children. Perfectionism, shame, and the fear of rejection have all gone hand-in-hand, revolving around my life in a vicious circle. I could not even recognize this during the first years of my entrance into motherhood, but slowly and surely, things started to get clearer and luckily the people in my life helped me to break free.

I am still on this journey till this day and will continue to be until I leave this earth. I am also certain that most moms feel this way, especially if our only influences are those moms we see on social media, in movies, or on TV—you know, the "perfect" moms who seem to have it all together all of the time and only experience victory after victory in their lives. If these are the only examples we are exposed to, this can feel really disheartening, especially when we find ourselves face-to-face with a reality that looks completely different from theirs. This is even more true, if we feel like we can't tell someone how we really feel.

This book was born out of a deep longing in my heart to change all of that. So, at the end of every chapter, I have put together some practical tips that you can start to implement today. I have gathered encouraging advice from my own life and the different sources who have really helped me through the years, as well as talked to other people to hear about their own experiences. This is in no way exclusive, and of course there are so many other things we could do or change in ourselves. But I want to focus on a few specific items, aiming to be as real and honest as possible in the process. If readers can grasp the importance of the things that we will discuss, I am sure there will be many more happy moms in this world!

I hope this book encourages you and helps you to relax more, enjoy more, and stress less! I also included practical tips that you can do daily to keep yourself encouraged and optimistic for the future. So, let's take this journey of imperfection together and accept ourselves just as we are: imperfect and perfectly flawed.

Chapter 1

"Everyone has everyday struggles."

When asked how her day was, one of my good friends once answered, "It's been one of those days where I have to survive. I just need to make it till bedtime!" My goodness, as I write this, today was one of those days. And if I'm even more honest, sometimes it feels like I'm going though seasons where it feels like *every* day is one of those days. Some days, I can breathe a little easier, but every day has its own struggles.

Every mom who has young children—especially if there are a few of them!—will attest to both the beauty and the pain that motherhood and parenting bring. I can definitely say that being a mom is both the most challenging thing I have ever been through, and yet also the most rewarding. To be honest, I really hoped that my life would be like the lives I followed on Facebook and other social media platforms. Or at least that motherhood for me would be just like I saw it was for the other moms around me. I never even stopped to think that maybe I was different, and that the things they struggled with or seemed not to be triggered by at all would be completely different for me.

As long as I can remember, I've loved children—as a child myself, I was always looking after the younger ones at family gatherings, and later as an adult. I was always so intrigued by them and I really loved their simplicity, their honesty, and of course, how cute they were! But I will never forget that horrid feeling deep in my soul when I watched my best friend and her baby and realized that I just didn't feel that way *all* of the time, so how would I ever be able to raise and love my own child? *There must be something wrong with me,* I thought. If only I knew then how far from the truth this really was.

The reality is that what we see when scrolling social media or during the short time we are around other moms, is only a glimpse of what is actually the truth of real life for them. One of my good friends once said that we should never compare someone else's highlights to our everyday fails and reality. We fall into the never-ending trap of comparing and competing and then feeling angry at ourselves, and don't forget the jealousy and discontentment! What we see on social media, at that social gathering, on the street, in the park, or at school, and wherever else you find yourself looking and comparing, is usually people on a good day, or at least they're trying to make it seem that way. If we're all really honest, most of us are just trying to put on a front that we are happy and that everything is "perfect." That's because, I think, most of us want people to see us that way. Because deep down, we all believe the lie that perfection and the perfect mom actually exist!

Even more importantly, we are so scared of rejection that we do everything to appear in control, happy, and positive so we don't experience that kind of pain again. I, for one, always find it so much easier to share my victories and my strengths compared with sharing my struggles and unveiling my weaknesses. But it's only by being real and raw and admitting that we are weak, that we can enter into true strength, lasting peace, and happiness. Pretending that we're not facing adversity does not help us get through it once it comes along anyway, and it sure as heck doesn't stop it from happening in the first place. We all struggle and we always will! Admitting it, sharing our struggles with others, and learning from it all are the things that actually get us through.

My children were all born about two years apart, and I was 27 when my third came along. This really was not the way I thought my life would turn out. I would never have imagined myself being a mother of three, and there being three of them all under four years old! But now, at twenty-nine, I've finally started to strengthen physically and started to grow—even if ever so slightly—emotionally and spiritually, and I can see so many things more clearly than I could even just two years ago. I am living proof that you don't have to have years and years of life experience, as it can take only one or two of these years to learn so many life-changing principles and see your perspective take a completely different turn.

Now, please don't misunderstand me; I have the utmost respect for the older and more experienced women in my life, and in no way do I count myself better or wiser than they. I have several women in my life who have walked this journey with me, who have years of life experience, and most of them even have adult children. They have all impacted me so much and shared their wisdom with me, which has many times probably saved my life. Because of the experiences of the women before me, I can share all that I have learnt and hopefully help the young women going after me. I want them to continue to learn even more, and experience even more joy and freedom in their journeys of motherhood!

Looking back now, I can see just how much I needed, and still need, all three of these children in my life. I didn't even know it, but they would be who God would use to get me to where I am today, and where I hope to be in the future. Without these children and the experiences, failures, and many lessons I have learnt so far, I would not be at the place I am today. In order to find who I was, in order to heal and be more confident in who I am, I needed to experience exactly what I did, how and when I did. I am so grateful for everything that God has given me, and I can say that I wouldn't change a thing!

Of course, I am still in the process of learning, and I know that we all are, in our own different ways. And the best part is that we will continue on this journey till the day we leave this beautiful earth. We are all imperfect, flawed, wounded, struggling, confused, lost, and overwhelmed. And yet we're also blessed, we're never alone, and we're all here for a reason. Every day is a new start; a new chance to improve; a new opportunity to learn; a new chance to say, "I'm sorry;" a new day to whisper, "I forgive you." It's a new day for memories, laughter, and love, every single day.

My aim is that everyone who reads this book will allow themselves to admit if they need help, acknowledge how they truly feel, and let go of the need for perfection in their lives. I have started to come to peace with who I am and what kind of mom I am, and my goal is that you will feel the same way, too. I am proud to call myself an imperfect, perfectly flawed mom. Are you?

PRACTICAL TIP #1:

What are you grateful for every day? Write down one thing you can be grateful for today, despite the negative things happening in your life, and hang it somewhere where you can always see it. Remind yourself of this when the day gets tough, even if that means every few minutes!

Chapter 2

"Let IT out and let THEM in."

I don't know why it still comes as a surprise to me, as I guess I probably should have expected this, but I am blessed with a child who seems to be the complete opposite of me. Every morning when I wake up, I need at least thirty minutes to just be quiet, to think, to pray, to sit in silence, and prepare myself mentally for the day ahead. I am an introvert, and my idea of fun and refueling is a cup of coffee with me, myself, and the sound of silence!

My son, however, is an extrovert who likes to talk…and shout and run around and scream! So, when he wakes up in the morning, he is ready to go and somehow full of information that he must have been storing and preparing all night. He is completely different from me and is ready to share everything with me the moment he steps into my room.

Until I realized that this is how he is, trust me, I went through every possible reaction possible. I felt frustration, confusion, I tried ignorance, I even tried shushing or walking away, until I finally started *listening*. I started to realize that I couldn't—nor did I want to—change him, and that these little talks were very important to him. Me hearing him out was the only way he felt was necessary to start his day. He needed me to listen to him so he could get out in the open everything he had been keeping inside. Children naturally seem to know that letting out their emotions always helps them to feel better in the long run. I wish we would all understand that, too.

Now, referring back to my son, most days I just smile and nod excessively as I listen to his random talks! It's important for me to embrace our differences and to love and accept him through them. But don't you think that in one way or another, this is true for all of us? That we often find ourselves with a child, a situation, a state of mind, or the reality of our lives in general, that seems to be the complete opposite of what we imagined it would be? Maybe it's the expectations of who we thought we'd be and the complete contrast to the person we see in the mirror today. Maybe your family, children, home, career, or the person you are is not what you would have ever thought to be your reality.

Whatever your truth may be, the good news is that all of this doesn't have to be a bad thing. You have not failed; you aren't a disappointment, and your situation is not something to regret or be ashamed of. Though everything may not be what you expected, it is nevertheless this way for a reason. This might just be your time to embrace something new, and to start a beautifully blessed journey no matter the ups and downs you may face. But in order for this journey to begin and end as a blessing, you cannot walk it alone.

I'm sure I'm not the only one who has realized that who I am as a mother today is not how I pictured myself in my late teens. Working in a nursery for five years and studying childcare in school made me feel like I would have it all in the bag when it was my turn to raise kids. I thought I would be the best and most prepared mom ever! However, what I was not aware of was that I was still incredibly young and full of deep emotional wounds and so many unmet personal needs. On top of that, I was tired, physically weak, and full of unattainable expectations and standards for myself and for others. Ultimately, this meant that reality was nowhere near what I had expected.

When my first child was born, I found myself struggling, and when my second came along, I thought I would feel this way forever. I started to think that this was just the way life would always be. I didn't realize how bad everything was then like I do now. Feeling the way I did seemed normal, and yet I felt a constant inward battle for something more. I knew that something wasn't right within me; all of those thoughts and feelings were just not the way I wanted to feel and I couldn't understand what was wrong.

It wasn't until I had my third baby that I realized how badly I wanted to do things differently and how much I needed something to change! I didn't want to cry and scream at my kids over spilt milk or cereal, I didn't want to feel so overwhelmed all the time, and most importantly, I didn't want to pretend that I was okay anymore. I knew I couldn't keep up this perfect façade for much longer.

The first thing I need to address—and this is very important for new moms to understand—is that in retrospect, I was suffering from mild post-natal depression after the birth of my second baby. I had the typical "blue" days for a little bit after my first was born, but with my second, I only realized something was really wrong when my mom came over to help one day. Everything she said or did seemed to frustrate me. I was starting to feel like I didn't feel anything anymore. I'd also lost my appetite and felt like I had no energy for anyone or anything.

I thought it was just from the exhaustion that comes with a new baby, but because this was true, and because this was a month or so after giving birth, it never even crossed my mind that it could be something more. I also didn't realize that although how I felt is quite common, it needed to be attended to right away.

A study from mentalhealth.org.uk shows that approximately 68% of women and 57% of men with mental health problems are parents, and the most common mental health problems experienced during pregnancy and after birth are anxiety, depression, and post-traumatic stress disorder (PTSD). In fact, 30 percent of women have experienced maternal-related anxiety, adjustment disorders, and stress.

(Mental Health 2021) Reading these statistics shocked me, because while I understood that three out of ten women (or one in five) could be suffering, we may have no clue that it's happening.

The biggest problem here is that most of us don't ever talk about this. And if you're anything like me, a drive for perfection definitely doesn't help. You see, if I only had lower expectations of myself and accepted that like other members of my family, I might be prone to mental health struggles, then maybe I would have taken it all a lot more seriously. But I was so adamant about overcoming these things on my own that I was able to just ignore the truth.

I always thought that accepting these kinds of issues was a sign of weakness or failure. But in reality, without acceptance, we are simply living in denial and we cannot get better and be free. Ignoring what your emotions are telling you is like pretending that you're not sick and hoping that your symptoms will just go away naturally. If you wouldn't ignore a broken bone, don't ignore your feelings or your mental state.

I was happy to accept the good but wanted to ignore the bad, hoping it would just go away. I thought I could do it all again tomorrow and be successful even if I had failed today. Eventually I recognized that refusing to address the truth only leads to more hurt in the long run. I realized that I didn't want to do it alone anymore and I didn't want to be who I had become.

The best part was that it didn't have to be this way! Deep down, I knew this to be true, but everything I had been told and taught by society and social media made me feel otherwise. I longed to hear the real-life stories of moms who felt the same way I did, to hear their struggles, their failures, and not just their triumphs! These are the women I went in search of, and these were the ones who surprised me and comforted me all the same. I was not alone! And you are not alone, either! We are not damaged, useless, or hopeless—we are imperfect, and this imperfection is exactly what makes us perfect.

Don't get me wrong, letting other people into my hurt and my struggles was one of the hardest, most shameful things I have ever had to do. But I will never forget the freedom I felt after one of the first times I shared my struggles with someone else. There is nothing more beautiful than failing time and time again yet having someone else remind you that you are not defined by your failures.

This doesn't mean we shouldn't improve and that we should allow ourselves to continue to hurt ourselves and the ones we love. But this helped me see that I was human, and that for us all, living up to our impossible standards is what's actually making us fail so often in the first place.

Hiding away when things get tough is also probably one of our most common reactions, as we naturally want to hide when we've done something wrong. Think about your child: when they do something they know is wrong, something they will most likely get in trouble for, what do they usually do? Unless they are old enough to be taught otherwise, they most likely try to hide! And even as adults, we tend to do the same, if you think about it. When things get tough, when we fail, when we feel down and discouraged, it is so much harder to tell someone, compared to when things are going great. It is our natural instinct to try to sort things out ourselves, to cover up the bad and the hurt, and then, once we think we have done enough, maybe we can share how we feel with someone else.

Sharing my struggles with someone I trust while in the midst of them has often saved me so much time and anguish and helped me figure out solutions. I can get on my way to healing so much faster. We don't need to wait till we're on the other side of our valley to ask for help or to tell someone we are struggling. And the more often we open up, the easier it gets and the less painful our downfalls become.

I think we are all in some way afraid of rejection, of how people will perceive us once we've told them how we really feel or what we've done. And this oftentimes holds us back from opening up and prolongs our time of suffering and confusion. But to my surprise, once I dared to step out and trust, only the opposite of my fears was true! I had to let go of so many things that I was holding onto, including my desire for perfection and being perceived as strong and brave, and accept that I am flawed, and that there are so many people out there just like me! You, too are not alone and if you're reading this, I am certain you are at the beginning of a beautiful journey. We are in this together. I promise.

PRACTICAL TIP #2:

Is there someone you can talk to and share something you are struggling with today? How did it make you feel after you did this? Try to practice this as often as you can and seek out people who will be supportive and understanding, people who will be there to listen and be safe for you to share with.

Chapter 3

"You were never meant to do it alone."

This chapter may be one of the longest in this book because we're going to cover something that has changed my life completely! And I really want other moms to grasp the importance of this, too.

If I'm really honest, some days I truly question why God gave me the life that He did. Why did He give me these children if it seems like I can't even cope? Some days I feel like I can't give anymore; I don't have the energy for that "one last story" or "one last hug." How on earth am I supposed to divide myself into so many parts, giving myself to three other small individuals, and have something left over for my husband, my other responsibilities, and, not to mention, myself?

Do you ever feel like that, too? But the real question is: do you feel ashamed to even admit it? And why is that? I can guarantee that every mom feels like this at least once in her parenting journey. The trouble is that not every one of these moms will admit it, let alone tell someone how she feels, or most importantly, ask for help!

I know for sure that I was one of those moms who thought she had to have it all together from day one. I thought I had to continue to do everything, just as I did before, that I could do it all by myself and I didn't need anyone's help because this was what I was made for. I would struggle to ask for my husband's help with the most mundane of things, and when my mom would come over, it would frustrate me because I felt like I should be the one doing all the things she was doing and that I shouldn't need her help.

This kind of mindset is what causes moms to burn out, to fall into cycles of addiction, to lose their strength, their health, and even their sanity. And, my friend, this is serious! We women really are gifted beyond words with the capacity to do so much, to juggle many tasks at once, and to wear as many hats as we see necessary. But we were not created to do it all alone.

If we go back to when my mom was a little girl forty or so years ago, growing up in a middle class or poor household, in order for a family to survive and to thrive, the mothers were most likely the heads of the households. If the fathers weren't as present as they could have been, the mothers had to do what was necessary in order to care for and protect their children. They most likely had no help—and no choice—and this sole responsibility on their shoulders was at times too much for them to handle. This generation of mothers may struggle to this day with control issues, submitting to their partners and husbands, letting their children be more independent, setting healthy boundaries, and feelings like depression, anxiety, and self-hatred. Deep down, the fact that they had no choice but to do it all alone may have made them angry, and they knew that eventually they might forget about taking care of themselves completely.

Another reason why I believe these women did it all alone was because that was what they were expected to do. If the majority of women raising families in their society and in their time were going through the same thing, and their mothers the same way before them, then it was inherently “the way it was” and “should be” and that was it. Having help, let alone asking for it, was abnormal, considered a privilege, and not something that was easily available, or for some, even an option.

With this kind of responsibility on someone's shoulders, life can get pretty tough. If it's all you know, it's all you will be living for, and it's all you will know yourself to be. These kinds of women then grow up still living their children's lives well into their adulthood, forgetting that they have their own lives to consider. This kind of control eventually drives their children and their grandchildren away as there is little room for innovation, uniqueness, and freedom for these women.

This kind of overt responsibility creates anxious, worried, scared, and ever-controlling women who deep down have too many regrets and too little joy in their hearts. I am sure that most of us would agree that this is not the kind of women and mothers we want to be!

Okay, maybe you didn't grow up in such a family but yet somehow, you find yourself following this exact pattern of behavior: taking control and feeling like you always have to do everything for everyone or else life will simply fall apart. This really is just our own expectation, or one that's been placed on us by society, our own family examples, or the people around us. But unfortunately, this is not a realistic and practical way to live your life! Interestingly enough, when you listen to what these older generations of moms say about their roles as mothers, most of the time you would hear things like, "It was so hard!" or "Children are such a struggle to raise, especially when they are so little!" They may not have realized it at the time, but for them, motherhood became a burden, and this is how they associate it even today!

Now, is this what I want people to hear when I talk about my journey of motherhood? Do I want to remember this period of my life as a struggle, full of hardship and pain? Or do I want to remember myself enjoying my children, their smiles, their laughter, and all the bits in between? The outcome is in our hands—what we want in the future, we create today.

If I want to have memories that I don't want to forget in the future and a relationship with my children even when they're older, I need to start making changes now. However, being the "perfect" mom is not about being "super-mom" (whatever that means) and it definitely doesn't mean you have to live solely for your kids and forget who you are in the process. If you have the opportunity to share your load, you have to take it! The best quote I could ever attach to this would be that it takes a village to raise a child, and this village is exactly what your children need!

Think about it: How much more beautiful, interesting, and memorable will your kids' childhood be if it is full of memories with people who loved and cared for them? How much more amazing would their memories be if they remembered people who were happy to be with them? Their parents well-rested and fulfilled and enjoying their lives? If you don't have grandparents or family members, that doesn't matter, so don't let this be an excuse!

Friends, neighbors, and anyone you can trust, especially if they are offering help, should be a part of your children's lives. Take these opportunities to let them spend time with other people, without you there, involved in every minute of their lives and learn to let go. Take this time to do whatever it is you need to do and share your load, even if that means you spend this time doing laundry and cleaning the toilets! Or just have that cup of coffee in peace and quiet at home and spend some time re-charging and focusing back on you.

Deep down, we have an innate longing for relationship, for companionship, to be helped and to help others. But to help others, and to be at our full potential, we need to learn to accept help from others first. We need to let go of our ego, our “I can do it all” mentality, and learn to let others take care of us. We need to let them share our loads so that one day, we don’t end up regretting trying to be and do more than we needed to. A happy mom really will mean happy children, and the only way you can do this job well is if you let others join in in this journey with you.

This leads me to something else I want to touch on that has a lot to do with our inability to ask for and accept help, and that is the subject of boundaries.

PRACTICAL TIP #3:

Organize and prioritize a day this week to spend some time alone or to go out with friends or family without your children! How did this make you feel during and after? If possible, plan this time out in your diary at least once a month and note down what changes you see in yourself as you learn to spend time with yourself.

Chapter 4

"Boundaries and people-pleasing."

Most of us have not only had an unhealthy example of boundaries in our own childhoods, but some of us seem to forget the importance or even the existence of boundaries. Boundaries are the parts of us that allow the good to come in and the bad to stay out. *(Cloud and Townsend 1992, 33)* This means that as moms, we need to learn and acknowledge what it is that is truly good for us and what is not. It's knowing when to say "yes" and when to say "no" and not feeling guilty about a decision we've made or feeling forced into doing something. This takes a lot of confidence and awareness of who we are and what is important to *us*, rather than to other people, including our children!

Boundaries mean that we learn to prioritize correctly, knowing when to do something and when not to. *(Cloud and Townsend 1992, 31)* Having them in our lives will mean that we need to let go of certain things such as perfectionism, expectations, and most importantly, control!

We also need to understand that not everyone will accept our boundaries, and this is a normal and, in fact, necessary part of our learning process. Sometimes we need to accept that our partners and our children may not want to accept our new "priorities" and we just need to accept their reactions without trying to fix things or fall back into old habits or ways of doing things. For example, if a friend or family member is shocked that you are suddenly asking for help and directly or indirectly implies that you "cannot handle" your own children, it would be very easy to subconsciously believe them and immediately retreat. In these moments, we need to remind ourselves of what is important and focus on that; in other words—don't take the bait! If these people are really able to help, we need to take it, no matter their push-back to your boundaries. Your boundaries may just be a way of shining onto them how much they themselves lack in this area, highlighting their own boundary issues that ultimately have nothing to do with you.

So, be prepared for the reality that people's reactions to our boundaries may take the form of anything from reluctance and manipulation to guilt and pure refusal. *(Cloud and Townsend 1992, 57)* No matter what someone else's reaction might be, our decision to ask for help and accept it is and always will be the right one both for us *and* our children. This will teach your children that it's okay to be weak and that it is necessary for us to share our loads with others. And most importantly, this will bring you so much more peace and be the best decision you make for both you and your kids in the long run!

Now, another reason we often tend to resist setting boundaries and prioritizing ourselves is because of the need to please the people around us. The best term for this is being a "people pleaser." Can you relate? This was definitely my story and to some extent, I am still fighting this today.

Often, in the beginning, people pleasing puts you on cloud nine, making you feel like you are such a kind person, that you are needed and very loved. It's almost like a constant elevation of your ego because people seem to like you so much and you're always "such a good person." But over time, most of us begin to realize that we can't please everyone and that one thing we may do to please one person may displease another. It becomes a never-ending cycle, a constant race where you can never really win. The best way I could describe people pleasing is like an overwhelming urge within you to seek the approval, applause, or "likes" of others. This usually means you quickly forget who you are and what *you* want for the sake of having other people like and act as if they value you.

However, the truth is that other people's opinions of you should not affect your value as a woman or as a mom! In other words, what other people say about us, how they react to us, and whether or not they like or approve of us does not and should not determine our value as people. If pleasing the people in our lives becomes more important to us than what *we* really want and need, eventually we will just be doing things out of obligation, not because we really want to! This “outward compliance” but “inward resistance” can lead to anger, and resentment *(Cloud and Townsend 1992, 54)* and affect the very relationships we are so eager to keep.

Saying “no” to your child and placing limits on how much you can handle and ultimately, placing yourself first are not signs that you are a bad mom! It does not mean that you are neglecting your child and his needs, and it surely does not mean that other people get to have a say about what you should or shouldn’t agree to! Many people think that saying “no” to someone is being rude, selfish, or unkind, but sometimes our “no” to someone else and our “yes” to ourselves can be the best thing we could ever do for both the other person and ourselves.

But here comes the other part of our problem: If you grew up in a dysfunctional family of any kind, your foundation for boundaries could be a really weak one. There's no surprise, then, that letting go of control and learning to say "yes" and "no" to the right things may seem as difficult as learning a new language. That's definitely how it was for me. If you grew up in a house where one parent was the boss, where that one voice was heard the loudest above everyone else's, and that person's way was eventually *the* way, I get it.

The culture I come from, as mentioned in Chapter 3, suffers from the lack of a healthy dynamic of what a husband and a wife or a father and a mother should be. Most of the families of my friends and people I know either grew up with an alcoholic, unemployed father and a mom who took care of the kids and worked full-time. Or, they had an absent father who worked but drank or socialized out of the house the rest of the time, leaving the mother at home and in charge of the finances, the children, and the roof over their heads. It seems that the pattern here is quite obvious—the women held the majority of the responsibility for the family and the children's everyday lives while the men held barely any. Now, remember, this was Eastern Europe in the 1980s and 1990s, and this is, of course, a generalization and my own personal experience. But even now, I am sure that many of us can attest to a very similar dynamic either in our own family or in many that we see today.

It is our responsibility to break free from the cycles and patterns of our parents, ancestors, and our culture and find our own healthy approach to parenting. Just because your family was imbalanced, dysfunctional, or had poor boundaries doesn't mean yours has to be the same way! I am certain that as moms, we get a new chance to do things over, to start a new family and new traditions that can impact not only our children, but the generations to come. Finding the perfect balance between being responsible *to* other people and *for* yourself is what makes the biggest difference toward being a happy and fulfilled woman and mother. It is the biggest difference between one that is always torn inside, seeking to be that "perfect" mom and one who is healthy, knows herself, her limits, and her strengths.

The perfect mom doesn't actually exist, but let's talk a bit more about where this idea of perfection comes from, shall we?

PRACTICAL TIP #4:

After reading this chapter, make a note of any areas of your life where you can identify the need to start setting boundaries. Do you struggle with people pleasing, and how do you think you will feel once you start to prioritize your wants over the opinions of others?

Chapter 5

"Busting the myth of perfection."

I never would have labelled myself a perfectionist. I knew I was organized and that I liked things done a certain way, but perfectionists just seemed too rigid. It seemed like these people were just too uptight compared to how I saw myself.

Now that I look back, I can see that perfectionism was so quietly woven into my DNA that I couldn't even see it! I was always so certain that I was just doing what was right and I thought that everyone placed these standards upon themselves, just like I did. It was only when I started to share my thoughts with other people that I realized that this perfectionism was actually about some deeper issues. These included things like the need for control, the fear of rejection and the opinions of other people, feeling overwhelmed and refusing to ask for help—all things we have discussed already in previous topics.

Here's a checklist that may help you recognize if you too have trouble dealing with perfectionism:

- Your mistakes are keeping you up at night.
- The high standards you have set for yourself and others are preventing you from experiencing true peace and joy.

- You are starting to feel a sense of lingering resentment or anger.
- You find yourself unable to accept those around you without wanting to change them in some way.
- You find yourself really struggling with control issues and letting go.

I have become more and more aware that perfectionists are not just the ones who make it obvious, but the ones who are quiet about it. These are the people who are silently judging everyone around them (and also themselves), those who find it hard to fall asleep at night because they are recounting the numerous ways they messed up that day, and the ones who get angry and frustrated at meaningless things, simply because they are so overwhelmed with trying to be in control all the time. I could definitely tick all three of these off, and most of the time, I blamed everyone around me, thinking *they* were just doing everything wrong when in reality, I was so full of unhealthy and unbalanced beliefs that I was spinning out of control.

Now, there is a very important difference I have to accentuate between striving to be a better person (i.e., doing better and achieving your goals) and perfectionism. They may seem very similar, but perfectionism has very different results. As Brené Brown so beautifully put it in her book *The Gifts of Imperfection*, striving for perfection is an unhealthy way of striving to meet standards and expectations that only you know exist, while all along, the most important thing to you is actually what people are going to think. *(Brown 2010, 71)* This is a constant striving to be perceived as perfect— it's all about what people will think or say about us, *(Brown 2010, 77)* so we end up pleasing others and searching for their approval and praise.

This kind of mindset eventually becomes like a prison, a place that you voluntarily put yourself into, a place that doesn't allow you to be free! It's the little voice that tells you that you can't ask for help, despite all the signs pointing to you being exhausted and overwhelmed, because people are going to think you're weak or incapable of looking after and raising your kids on your own. It's the little gremlin that sits on your shoulder and makes you constantly criticize and compare yourself to all the moms you know because they seem to be doing everything so much better than you, whatever that may be. It doesn't leave room for mistakes, it doesn't allow you or others to be their true selves, and it doesn't allow you to genuinely feel what you really feel for fear you may be rejected in the process.

I've also noticed that perfectionism has many levels, and with every new season of life, we may start to see the layers unveil themselves one by one. I remember how I started remembering moments that would drive me crazy, such as people making small mistakes, acting immorally, making what I thought were bad choices. Then, I turned my irritation to little things like my husband's tidying habits and his input about where things should be around the house.

The first moment in motherhood that made me realize I was struggling with this was when I gave birth to my first child and I was stressing out over not being able to keep the house tidy when we had our first visitors after we brought our baby home. I remember feeling so overwhelmed that I didn't have enough energy to make the house spotless before the guests' arrival. Writing this out sounds so crazy to me! But at that point, my need for perfection was completely overtaking me and I just felt helpless.

Later, the struggle increased even more when I realized just how much my children's misbehavior triggered me. I just couldn't cope with them not listening, especially in public, and though I tried my best to hide it, it would drive me crazy when I was alone with them at home. This was all because of this same perception of perfection that I wanted so badly to uphold. If they didn't listen, I felt like I was a bad mom. If they were acting up, I took their behavior as a reflection of my own worth and value as a mother. There were some impossible standards I had set for them in my mind, and when they didn't live up to them, I just didn't know what to do and couldn't bear to not be in control.

After my other two were born, my triggers would evolve into something else, but in all honesty, it all came down to the same obsessive need to be "the best." I had to have the best-behaved kids, to look the best, and this no longer applied just to the thoughts and opinions of the people around me. I soon realized that I could be alone or with just the children and yet I was still driven by this same need, because now, it was no longer just the opinion of others that mattered but also my own. This standard was so deep within me that the critical voices I kept hearing no longer had to come from the people around me; they now came from me, too.

You see, the first step to overcoming this perfectionistic mindset is accepting responsibility for this way of thinking. Though this may have been learned, or it was how you were raised or how other people told you to live, no one is to blame and none of this really matters. This is so important! So many of us live our lives not even knowing why we are the way we are and disliking ourselves along the way. Our families may have shaped us and instilled in us that unhealthy need to be perfect, but this is not necessarily who we truly are. In the end, you and you alone are responsible for what you think and how you act and what kind of life this leads to. So, take responsibility for what's going on within *you*.

Then you must decide that you want to make a change and that you cannot and will not live with these constant expectations you have placed upon yourself and other people.

Thirdly, you must stop blaming, judging, and criticizing yourself and others! You must accept and admit that you *will* make mistakes, and that you are flawed, imperfect, and ultimately, human. You were not created to be perfect, and the best way you will grow and reach your full potential is by failing and trying again, over and over.

Something that is equally important is deciding to stop comparing yourself to other people. This truly is a decision and one you may need to make again and again every day. Accepting who you are and embracing the uniqueness of you and your children while no longer trying to change yourself or anyone around you will truly set you free! If need be, take a break from social media, or avoid going to places or meeting people that may trigger you or make you feel less than you really are. It is much better to do this for a short time than continue to trigger yourself and prolong your healing process. This could be so helpful while you retrain yourself and learn to let go of all these perfectionistic standards in your mind. You can return to these things and people once you are ready.

And lastly, but probably most importantly, you need to allow yourself to be who you are and feel exactly what you are feeling. These perfectionistic gremlins tell us that what people will think of us if we express certain emotions is much more important than being real, and this is a straight up lie! Suppressed feelings and the outward façade of perfection ultimately lead to anxiety, *(Brown 2010, 72)* unexpected bursts of anger, rage, aggression, and depression, and ultimately, so, so many regrets. *(Cloud Townsend 1992, 226)* This is serious, and if you cannot allow yourself to be real, you will find it even harder to accept the people around you.

If you want to be a happy, healthy mom, then it all starts with you being authentic, admitting when you are wrong, learning to say sorry, and showing your children that being authentic, loving, and accepting of others is truly what matters. Doing everything "right" is not what matters at all! Talking about your struggles with perfection is truly the only way to bust the myth of perfection for good.

PRACTICAL TIP #5:

Write down several ways you have allowed yourself to believe the lies of perfectionism. Where and when do you think this came from? What areas do you struggle with the most? What areas do you feel like you could change even today, and what things do you need more time to focus on? Spend some time expressing your emotions today, whether through talking, drawing, dancing, exercising, or even screaming! Let yourself feel what is in your heart!

Chapter 6

"Keep things simple."

I think it's safe to say that perfectionism is a trap and usually doesn't simplify our lives, but on the contrary makes them so much more difficult. It makes you feel like you are okay because you are in control, or that it's okay because tomorrow you will have a new chance to do better and reach whatever standards you were trying to reach (and failed to) today. It can be like a false sense of hope and lull you into thinking that you're just striving to "be your best self," but deep down, you're living in pure chaos. Remember, perfection is all about perception and wanting to look like we are thriving, like we're okay, and that everything is under control. *(Brown 2010, 77)* In reality, we're not allowing ourselves to be real; we're most likely over-complicating things and stopping ourselves from enjoying our lives in the process.

Other areas in which we have to let go of striving to be perfect are things like thinking that we will be the perfect mom if our children only ever eat healthy homemade food, they have no screen time, we always keep our house clean and never have messes. Again, if we're really honest, it's not that we know we will be perfect, but that people will *think* we are. Inwardly, we are striving for and hoping that other people will praise us for being such good moms because we are making the best decisions for our kids.

I, personally, have always wanted my children to have fresh home-cooked meals, to be playing with wholesome toys, doing crafts all day, and for the house to look picture perfect all the time. But, with a teething baby, an emotional whirlwind of a two-year-old and an active, independent four-year-old all on my plate almost 24/7, I realized quickly that I had to get my priorities straight—these goals were just not physically possible.

There were some days that I didn't have the energy to cook, or clean, or keep thinking of new activities for my little ones. And the truth is that all of us have these days, and that's okay! On these days, my kids would have cereal for breakfast and dinner, and plain pasta for lunch, and watch cartoons more than once during the day. And almost to my own surprise, they were even happier because they were fed and busy, and I was happier, too because this left me more time to relax and focus on the youngest. You see, I had to make the decision as to what was more important: Was it a hot meal, or meeting my children's needs and respecting my own ability to handle the situation that day? I needed to learn to keep things simple.

Sure, I could have made that hot meal, or organized those fun activities for them, but I most likely would've exploded and lost my peace in the process if it was one of those tougher days. I needed to put peace, joy, and comfort for myself and my children at the top of my priority list and everything else had to come after. Of course, it's undeniable that eating healthy, home-cooked meals is a very good thing to want for your family, and to try to uphold it as much as we can. But the reality is that the meal can wait for another day if it has to, and so can the dishes and the laundry and everything in between. Your peace is what matters most.

If food and screen time aren't triggers for your need for perfection, then what about messes? If you type "mess" into an online thesaurus, this is what you see: clutter, chaos, confusion, mayhem, and eyesore, to name a few. Eyesore? This is exactly what I think of when I step into any kind of mess in my house! The whole process of cleaning and having to constantly put things away and tidy up toys was a very big trigger for me as my children got older, and it was especially difficult for me to relax whenever we had any guests. Does this sound familiar? The perfectionists within us could not stand anyone seeing our house less than perfect as this would again put us at risk of being rejected or labelled as something negative.

I was raised by a very organized and tidy mom, so keeping things in order and clean is in my DNA and something I am really happy I have learnt from her. However, I started to notice that this need for order also drove me to a scary need for control. To this day, I notice that if I am stressed, angry, or feeling overwhelmed, I immediately start to see every toy and every little thing that is out of its place and it accelerates my anxiety within seconds. The more out of control I feel with my children, the more I want to control the environment around me. This chaos that I see on the outside becomes unbearable because it starts reflecting the chaos that's on the inside, too. I don't know how many times I have started cleaning and tidying when I have felt stressed. I remember one time when I was so nervous to do a talk that I started to clean my shoes—I was doing it without even thinking!

However, I have started to learn that if the daily messes and chaos that my young children create begin to irritate me, my first point of contact is to check within myself as to what else is bothering me. This may just be a trigger that's pointing to a deeper issue that I need to sort out before I start dealing with what I am seeing in front of me. Even practical tips like creating a rule that doesn't allow toys to be taken into the main communal areas of the house can help to avoid so many arguments! Another solution could be teaching your children to tidy up and pack away their toys after themselves and telling them how you feel about the messes they make. Of course, they need to be old enough to understand, but even toddlers quickly learn these things from their siblings and can be taught to clean up their toys, too. But again, the focus has to be on dealing with our own issues so that eventually even the biggest of messes won't trigger any perfectionism alarm bells within us.

Now, one thing I want to stress that is important for healthy boundaries and to help your perfectionism is that communal areas or your personal bedroom and your children's rooms are very different things. As parents, we should learn to respect and accept the boundaries of our children's personal space. If a child has their own room, we need to learn to let go and stay out of it! Sure, it is also our responsibility to teach them to be responsible and to organize their things so they don't break or lose them. But just like we wouldn't like our friends or family members coming into our bedroom and telling us what it should look like, or that we should be doing this or that, we need to leave space for our children to be free to do the same with their space and their choices.

This is especially true if our correction and nagging is becoming detrimental to our relationship with them. When your children grow up, do you want them to remember your love for them, or your anger and frustration about the messes they made and your need to be in control? Just because your child's bedroom is a mess, it does not mean you have to go and clean it up, and it doesn't mean that this reflects on you as being a bad mother! This, again, is the perfectionism and the perception thereof that is talking. Letting go of this control and the need to have every area of our lives looking and being perfect will eventually free you to see that there really are more important things in life than just a picture-perfect house!

Another way we can simplify our lives is by being more flexible and trying to let go of our beloved plans. This is easier said than done! Planning is actually a very wise thing to learn to do, especially with very young children, but when it comes to the reality of the day, sometimes our plans just aren't working and a wise parent would take this as a cue to change things up. I struggle with this still, and I know first-hand that some days, letting go of our plans can be so hard to do! For example, if you had planned to stay at home that day and do some chores around the house and yet your children seem to be bouncing off the walls because they need some fresh air, it would save you a whole lot of aggravation in the long run if you put your plans aside and took them out for a walk or to your local park. I know how hard this can be when there are piles of things to be done! But sometimes, we just need to reprioritize and learn to be more flexible and we will be so much happier in the long run.

While we're on the subject, getting your kids and yourself outside, even if you feel like you have to force everybody out of the door, can be the remedy to so many problems you may be facing. Sometimes we can feel anxious, hopeless, and stuck simply because we have been inside the house for too long, and because our brains just physiologically need more oxygen to function. According to mind.org.uk, oxygen is essential in maintaining healthy brain function, growth, and healing, and spending time in nature has been found to help with mental health problems, including anxiety and depression! *(Mind 2018)* A simple fifteen-minute walk outside or running around in your back garden can be the proverbial difference between life and death for your body, your emotions, and even your relationships with your children!

The opposite is true as well. If your plans were to spend time outside or to go to the shops to buy some food, and your children are having a complete meltdown, or you feel overwhelmed even before you leave the house, maybe staying at home is what you really need. It would be so much better for you to readjust your plans and prioritize your peace and your children's needs rather than sticking with your plan, no matter how much you wanted or even needed to leave the house that day! Sometimes, we just need to remind ourselves to breathe and to keep things simple.

Perfectionism can make things seem so complicated at times. It wants us to keep striving, to keep going, to keep up the act that everything is fine, and to have no time to even stop and think about what we truly want and need! Because the perfect mom would make things work regardless, right? Or she would never be late, have a messy house, allow her kids to leave their rooms looking like a bomb hit them, cancel a meeting with her friends at the last minute, or go outside to the local park in her joggers unprepared...right?!

If we would just allow ourselves to calm down and breathe and truly think in those moments, we would know deep down what it is we need to do. It's up to us to silence that inner critical voice, to keep things simple, to trust ourselves, and to do what will be best for everyone!

PRACTICAL TIP #6:

How can you make your life simpler today? Decide to do one thing differently today than you normally would and let yourself be imperfect. Think about how it made you and your children feel, and how much simpler life would be if you implemented this into other areas of your parenting.

Chapter 7

"Change what you can, accept what you can't."

Most of us have probably heard of the serenity prayer, often used in sobriety programs. It goes something like this: "God, grant me the serenity to accept the things I cannot change, the courage to change the things I can, and the wisdom to know the difference."

Even if this has no connotations to sobriety for us personally, it's still something I think we all need to remember and repeat aloud from time to time because of just how powerful a statement it really is.

One of the biggest struggles in life is probably accepting other people and situations for what they are without trying to change them in any way, shape, or form. At first, it could be accepting your parents, then your friends, then your partner, and lastly, your children—all of whom we try to change because we just can't fully accept them for who they naturally are. Changing a new top to a different one is easy—if you don't like it, you can just swap it for something else. But trying to change a person in the hopes of swapping out the parts of them you dislike for something you do like or that would be easier for you to handle is not our responsibility, our decision, or even our right!

This might be hard for us to hear, especially when our situation may seem like an easy fix if that person would just change something about how they are. However, it's much harder to accept when our attempts to change the ones we love don't work and we cannot come up with a quick and easy solution, and the situation just isn't changing for the better. I have found myself in the middle of similar dilemmas so many times in my life, especially with my husband and children. I often so desperately want to fix things and make them better (this is where perfectionism also plays its tricks on me) that I quickly jump to the role of trying to change the very nature of who these people are. And this, unfortunately for the perfectionist in me, is not my job; it never was, and it never will be!

Just think about it: How many times have we as moms believed that it's our job to "help" our child in one area or another, or to be the one to fix things? In reality, maybe we were actually aiming to change their behavior or a character trait that we found too hard to handle?

Now, of course we all know how important it is to help shape a child's character, to teach them right from wrong, harmful behavior from positive behavior. However, I am referring to issues such as tidy rooms, food choices, playing outside or inside, messy play or building with blocks, and everyday clothes or pajamas. Sometimes, we are so set in our ways of how things should be, or how we were taught they should be, that we don't allow our children to have any freedom or to experience the natural consequences of their choices.

Sometimes, it might just seem easier to stick to your ideas and ways of doing things, and almost force this upon our spouses or children rather than letting them be who they are and do what they choose. And trust me, I get it! It might be easier to get out the door, keep your house clean, and make sure your children eat healthy meals if you do everything your way! But sometimes, it's not actually what may seem easier that is better for us, and in reality, a change of perspective and allowing the people around us to just make their own choices becomes the simpler and more peaceful option for everyone.

When we are set in our ways and we strive to change things so they happen the way *we* want them to, in essence, what we're doing is trying to change the people next to us to become another version of ourselves. What we're saying is, "If you're like me, then things are easy, but if you're different, well, that's when things start to get tough."

We've all thought this at one point or another. And have you noticed that it's usually so much easier to understand and accept your child who is in many ways similar to you? And yet, it's so much harder to accept the child who is your complete opposite, secretly wishing, "If only you were more like me!"

We might not admit it, but it's normal to desire being in control and having things happen the way we believe they should and then in turn, trying to change whatever is the opposite, even if this is our beloved little child. But the good news is that the quicker we realize this, the easier it will be to accept our differences and find ways to adapt so that everyone is happy. For example, if your child hates tidying up her toys, you have to stop trying to make her into her sibling who always seems to have a clean room. Undoubtedly, both of your children have been taught the same responsibilities, but trying to change the messy one into the tidy one will just be a pointless effort that really isn't necessary. Or, forcing your sense of style onto your child (or even your partner!) when he wants to wear something different because your way is more appropriate or correct, rather than seeking to find a compromise or just allowing him to experiment.

These examples may seem logical now, but in the heat of the moment and when arguments or issues are constantly recurring, it can be really hard to see the bigger picture and stop yourself from trying to change the people around you. If you can't change something, and you have been shown numerous times that this is a battle that's not worth fighting, let it go! Put down your weapons, your understanding, your knowledge, your experience, and just let people be who they are.

I've found that the more we try to change and control others, the more they push back, and the longer the problem goes on. Sometimes the best thing we can do for people is to just let them do whatever it is they want to do and let them experience the natural consequences of their choices. And to our surprise, they might eventually end up coming back and choosing what we advised in the first place! But instead, we have allowed them to be free in this process and kept our peace and our relationship intact.

No one wants to be controlled or to feel like they aren't accepted the way they are. No one wants to feel like they're not enough, or that they're constantly making the wrong decisions. We have to allow our children and our partners to be free in making their own choices and to learn to let go of trying to fix and change things for whatever we deem to be "better."

Another thing I have noticed is just like with my urge to clean and keep things tidy when I am inwardly stressed or overwhelmed, the same goes for when I find myself desperately trying to fix and change the people around me. The more anxious I feel because of things that I am not dealing with inwardly, or if I am feeling overworked, overloaded, or overtired, the more likely I am to start trying to control the world around me.

If you are not prioritizing yourself and your needs, both emotional and physical, then it will be much harder for you to think clearly and see the needs of your children or your spouse. If you are feeling neglected by your partner and deep down you are craving their attention and spending time on your relationship, then you are more prone to nagging, pointing out faults, being negative, and demanding that they change. Whereas if you are well-rested, you've had your "me time," and expressed your desire to spend some quality time together and had this need met, then it will be much easier to accept your partner as they are and be happy and content. The more we try to change people, the less content we will become, and most likely, the more they will push back or run away from us. And the more we prioritize ourselves and stop trying to do everything ourselves, the easier it will be to accept those around us just the same.

As I write this, I have recently been reminded of this truth, yet again, through my attempts at setting some boundaries. As mentioned before, boundaries are about us and about what we will or will not accept, and changing our behavior to demonstrate this. However, I quickly went from changing my own behavior to demanding that the other person change theirs in order for this situation to be fixed in one way or another because, "I said so, and this is my boundary."

If you, too have struggled with boundaries your whole life, this will be very understandable for you. Placing boundaries for your sake and trying to change the person you're placing them on are two very different things.

In fact, boundaries mean that we are finally giving up control and beginning to love. The only person we do end up taking control over is ourselves! *(Cloud and Townsend 1992, 164)* Oh, what a freeing thought that is! We aren't expected to have total control over our children and their mistakes, and their poor choices aren't a reflection of who we are as women, or as mothers. Letting go of this anxiety and pressure on ourselves is how I believe we were actually made to live!

PRACTICAL TIP #7:

What areas are you constantly trying to change in your family life, or maybe even in your children? How can you let go of control and let them experience their individual freedom in these areas? Write these down somewhere where you can see them daily as a reminder to let go and let love!

Chapter 8

"Healing and hope for the future."

As I have written this book, I have often thought back to how much I have changed and healed on this journey of motherhood. Although my journey is really only just beginning, the lessons I have learnt and the ways I myself have changed as an individual and as a mother give me hope that there is still so much more freedom and joy in store for me in the future.

Things have become easier the more I have surrounded myself with people and resources that have widened my understanding of myself and the characters of my children. There is a vast amount of practical advice available for parenting. The most important thing I have come to see is that the more I allow myself to focus on my own reactions and my own hurts when facing challenges in motherhood—rather than focusing on what the child is doing and the situation in front of me—the better I've been able to cope with these challenges.

Now, don't get me wrong, this in no way means that motherhood is always easy and that you will never feel overwhelmed! On the contrary, life will probably be both harder and more amazing than you could have ever imagined. But I truly believe that our children are given to us as gifts and as tools for change—change both in ourselves and our own characters, and the change that they themselves will bring to this world in their lifetimes.

It is always those closest to us who bring out the best *and* worst in us, correct? And so, if life doesn't shape us through our relationships with our partners, friends, or family members, it will most definitely happen through our children! So far, though these have been the most painful times of my life, I have never regretted a single one of these moments because of the results I can see in my life afterward. This is something I would not have achieved if it wasn't for the people in my life, including my children.

You see, it is our children who bring us back to our own childhood, our own memories, and our own way of reacting to things. And if we don't understand in those moments that they are just that—children—we can easily begin to act and react based on our own experiences and trauma. When we become parents, we often find ourselves either doing the complete opposite of what hurt us the most about our own childhood or turning into the very people we vowed we would never become. We can even begin hearing ourselves speaking the exact words we heard our parents say or treating our children just as we were treated, whether this was good or bad. I don't think this is something anyone can avoid, but what we can do is heal from these things and set new trends and behaviors for both the benefit of our own future and that of our children.

Let's stop and think about this for a second. What kinds of things have you told yourself you would never do? Or what kinds of cycles have you found yourself in? Maybe you are constantly striving to be better than your parents were, or provide more for your children than you ever had as a child?

Of course, we are not talking about traumatic and damaging behaviors such as abuse when talking about these kinds of internal vows. Abuse should never be justified, and these types of behavioral cycles should be broken if we find ourselves repeating them.

Help, healing, and forgiveness could be the best and the only way forward from this kind of trauma.

But in this case, striving for a better future and having a desire for your child to have a better life than you did as a child are not bad things in and of themselves. Here we are thinking about the moments where, if we are truly honest with ourselves, we have let our past experiences and the hurt they caused us shape the way we treat our children, the choices we make, and what our lives have become. For example, maybe for you, it's the need to provide your children with more than you had as a child. Though this is understandable, it could end up being the very thing that causes the most damage to your children, making them ungrateful, spoilt, and unprepared for the real world when they reach adulthood. Poverty and lack of basic necessities and the comparison and alienation from society because of these can be very painful for a child to experience. But your past does not have to define your parenting style and your life today; you can set healthy patterns for both yourself and your children.

Or maybe you had controlling parents who never allowed you to make your own decisions, or parents who excessively tried to protect you from danger or from getting hurt, and thus stopped you from experiencing life to the full. These kinds of experiences can either mold us into the very thing we feared, or make us the very opposite, and in either case, it can be just as damaging to our children. What they really need is balance, and it is pointless for us as parents to try to fix our external situations and problems without first looking inside of ourselves. We sometimes don't even realize how much power we have and how we affect our children, seemingly without even doing anything. And interestingly enough, our children are a reflection of our inner selves much more than we know.

I cannot tell you how many times I have been beside myself trying to find ways to help my child with a certain behavior, trying to find a solution, that I was so focused on my child I didn't even realize that all along, the problem was actually with me! By fixing my own reaction to the situation and the child, my child's behavior changed automatically. More often than not, the things that hurt us now are most likely the things that have hurt us before. *(Cloud and Townsend 1992, 262)* This is just another way of showing us that our wounds are still there, and that we need to do something about them if we want to live a fulfilling life!

Again, we can't control what other people say or do, but we can control our reactions to them, and our behavior should never be excused based on the blame we put on other people for the way they have treated us. We are our own responsibility, but as parents, we become responsible *to* our children as well. *(Cloud and Townsend 1992, 32)* Letting go of our anger and hurt means we can finally break free from those behaviors that we so strongly want to change. And though it might seem unfair and extremely difficult to forgive our parents or others who have hurt us, it is the only way we can truly be free.

By forgiving the people who have hurt us in the same way that now our child is hurting us, not only will our child's behavior not affect us anymore, but we will be able to deal with it in a completely different way, meaning the outcome will be different, too. Sure, we cannot condone their behavior, and we should never just accept that it is okay, but we cannot hold onto it, constantly blaming them for what they've done.

However, knowing what to do doesn't mean that it will be easy...no way! Sometimes this process takes days, months, and even years. But the more you go through this process, the easier it becomes and the more freeing it is to admit our own faults and our own unforgiveness and take responsibility for ourselves and stop blaming other people! This doesn't mean that we will never be hurt by the things our children do because feeling hurt is a normal part of life. This just means that hopefully you will now have the right tools to use when these kinds of situations come your way.

The reason I write all of this is because we have touched on so many issues in this book that may be hindering us from truly being the moms we were created to be, the moms we want to be. And sometimes, it may feel like we can try everything and follow all the tips (even the ones in this book!) and yet we still feel like we're going nowhere. Usually, this is because of the issues that I outlined above—that we are still holding onto things that happened in our own childhoods that are preventing us from moving forward, accepting ourselves and our children, and being the parents we so desperately desire to be. To be honest, most of the time, the issues we struggle with that come up so evidently in our parenting, such as perfectionism, control, trying to be strong, failing to ask for help, and not prioritizing ourselves, could all be coping mechanisms or simply woven into our DNA from our experiences in childhood. The only way to deal with these issues *now* is to go back to *then*.

I understand how painful this can be, but the road to healing and to a truly amazing life is never easy. If we want to achieve these victories, we need to deal with these inner issues; otherwise, they will eventually come to the surface regardless, if not in our lives but in the lives of our children and our children's children. If this is not the future we want, then change starts with us, now!

Finally, I wanted to remind you that you alone know what is—or is not—right for you and your family. Sometimes, perfectionism creeps into our lives simply through the words of other people; their opinions, judgments and comments can make us second-guess our choices. Guard your heart! There are no set rules that we can all follow because what works for me may not work for you. Let your children's individuality along with your values and beliefs be your guide, not other people's opinions.

You know, the most amazing moms I know are not the ones who have it all together, whose children are always well behaved, and the ones who are always calm, patient, and happy. They are the ones who follow their hearts, who are real, who are able to say sorry and admit they are wrong and set boundaries for themselves and their children. They are constantly in the process of changing their own hearts and beliefs rather than just the situations around them.

We all have these kinds of moms in our lives, but sometimes, we may find it hard to see them because we are so focused on the models of motherhood that our culture tells us to idealize. Sometimes we don't even look at those moms because they are so different to us, or at least they seem that way. Or even worse, we frown upon them and call them names. But deep down, we might be longing to be even a slight bit like them because of how free they really are.

I was one of these frowning moms. I thought that being a mother involved so many different things, but only when I became one myself did I start to realize that most of these things were all worthless. Now, there is nothing more admirable than a mom who is willing to admit that she struggles, who is constantly looking within herself at her motives and her heart, and one who doesn't fit the mold of society or perfectionism.

She is free. She is not perfect. And in fact, most of the time, these moms are perfectly flawed. But she is happy, her children are happy, and she is at peace.

One thing is for certain, there is healing and hope for our future—for all of us perfectly imperfect moms.

PRACTICAL TIP #8:

Feel free to use the "Notes" pages to write down your thoughts, ideas or even revelations! I hope they serve you well, for whenever you need them in the future!

References

Brown, Brené, 2020. *The Gifts of Imperfection*, (71-72, 77). London: Vermilion.

Cloud, Henry and Townsend, John, 1992. *Boundaries*, (31-33, 54, 57, 164, 226, 262). Grand Rapids: Zondervan.

Mentalhealth.org.uk, 2021. *Mental health statistics: family and parenting*. https://www.mentalhealth.org.uk/statistics/mental-health-statistics-family-and-parenting

Mind.org.uk, 2018. *Nature and mental health*. https://www.mind.org.uk/information-support/tips-for-everyday-living/nature-and-mental-health/how-nature-benefits-mental-health/

……Notes……

......Notes......

......Notes......

......Notes......

www.ingramcontent.com/pod-product-compliance
Ingram Content Group UK Ltd.
Pitfield, Milton Keynes, MK11 3LW, UK
UKHW020420250726
13967UKWH00007B/2734